The Country Kitchen Library

Making Ice Cream, Ices & Sherbets

by Phyllis Hobson

Garden Way Publishing
Pownal, Vermont 05261

Cover design & drawing by Susan Eder
Line drawings by Carol MacDonald

Fifth printing, July 1984
Printed in the United States by Alpine Press

Library of Congress Cataloging in Publication Data
Hobson, Phyllis.
    Making your own ice cream, ices, and sherbets.

    Includes index.
    1. Ice Cream, ices, etc. 2. Desserts, Frozen.
I. Title.
TX795.H67   641.8'62   77-4714
ISBN 0-88266-105-1 pbk.

CONTENTS

INTRODUCTION

Ice cream can be a most elegant dessert to serve guests or it can be just a simple snack at bedtime. It can be a special treat topped with chocolate sauce and chopped nuts; it can be scooped lavishly onto a fruit pie; or it can be served in a sugar cone to hungry children.

This most popular of American desserts — and its near relatives, the sherbets, ices, parfaits and mousses — is not only one of the simplest of fine foods to make, it also is one of the most nutritious. It is a delicious way of including milk and eggs in one's diet and — with the sherbets and ices — may include a variety of healthful and tasty fruits and nuts.

Since the days of the Roman Empire, when emperors and their courts ate snow, brought from the Alpine passes and flavored with fruit juices, a great many variations on the original recipes have been developed throughout the western world.

Some of the many basic ways of making ice cream include such long-accepted types as: Philadelphia Ice Cream, French Ice Cream, Italian Ice Cream, New York Ice Cream, Frozen Custard, Rennet Ice Cream, Gelatin Ice Cream, Marlow and Frozen Pudding. We've included three basic recipes — vanilla, chocolate and strawberry — for all nine types of ice cream, plus 36 variations you can use with all of them.

Ice cream's second cousins — the sherbets, ices, parfaits and mousses — are somewhat lower in calories, less expensive and simpler to make. We've included several recipes for each of these.

And, for the most elegant of all desserts, when time and expense are no object, we offer some really special recipes for Baked Alaska, Bombe, Frozen Brule, Frozen Plum Pudding, Spumone and Tortoni.

FREEZING EQUIPMENT

**YOU'LL
NEED:** One of the following:

Hand-cranked freezer — These old reliable ice cream freezers date back to before George Washington's time. They consist of an outer bucket or tub made of wood, metal or plastic which holds the ice and salt. Inside this is an inner container which holds the mixture to be frozen. The ice should be crushed and mixed well with rock salt (one part salt to eight parts ice). The salt acts to lower the temperature of the ice, which freezes the cream mixture. As the container is rotated by the crank, a dasher inside the inner container also agitates the freezing mixture and makes the ice cream smooth and creamy by keeping it from forming large crystals.

Electric freezer — Motor-driven ice cream freezers are identical to the hand-cranked models except that the crank which rotates the inner tub and the dasher are turned by an electric motor.

Ice cream maker — No rock salt or ice is needed with an electrical ice cream maker, which fits into the freezing compartment of the home refrigerator or a food freezer. The motor-driven dasher stirs the mixture and keeps it smooth while the temperature provided by the freezing compartment freezes it.

3

Refrigerator trays — Ice cube trays or other shallow metal trays also may be used to freeze ice cream in the home freezer or the freezing section of the refrigerator. Since there is no stirring action provided during freezing, it is necessary to remove the mixture from the freezer when it is partially frozen and whip it by hand or with a mixer until it is smooth. Then it is returned to the freezer and allowed to freeze solid.

Homemade freezer — If you have none of the above special equipment available, homemade ice cream can be made by lining the bottom of a large container with a mixture of salt and ice, inserting a smaller container which holds the mixture to be frozen, then pouring more ice and salt around the sides and over the top. The inner container should have a tight-fitting lid and the mixture will need to be stirred occasionally.

One variation of this method, which works very well and makes good use of an obsolete utensil, is to make ice cream in what your grandparents called a *fireless cooker.* This is a heavily insulated contrivance which was used as a slow-cooker in the 1920s by heating a flat stone and the kettle of food on the kitchen stove. Then both were placed down in the insulated well to continue cooking by their own heat. Many of these old fireless cookers are still around.

To make ice cream, the cooker well can be lined with the salt and ice mixture and the kettle filled with ice cream mixture. The inner container should be turned occasionally, and it makes for a smoother product if the ice cream is stirred with a spoon at least once during the freezing process.

GENERAL DIRECTIONS

Rapid freezing is needed to make smooth frozen desserts in the refrigerator's freezer area. Ice cream made in crank-type ice cream freezers and with the new refrigerator ice cream makers, on the other hand, is best frozen at a moderate rate which will give the mixture time to swell. Since ice creams and sherbets fluff up from the dasher agitation, a given recipe will produce a larger volume when it is frozen with agitator action than when left in a refrigerator tray.

When freezing desserts in refrigerator trays, the mixture should be frozen to a fairly solid consistency, then removed to a chilled bowl and beaten until it is fluffy. Then quickly return it to the freezer area to continue freezing. This method is not used, however, with molded desserts such as Parfait, Bombe or Spumone, which never are stirred.

To insure rapid refrigerator freezing, the temperature should be turned to its lowest point about one hour before preparing the mixture. But with electrical ice cream makers used in the refrigerator, follow the manufacturer's directions.

For crank-type ice cream freezers — electrical or hand-turned — a ratio of one part rock salt to eight parts ice is needed. Finely crushed ice melts faster and freezes the ice cream better. About 20 pounds of ice is needed to freeze and "ripen" one gallon of ice cream or sherbet.

For either method, it is important to use no more sugar

than the amount specified in the recipe, for too much sugar keeps the mixture from freezing properly. Be careful, too, to avoid overbeating the egg whites and whipping cream. They should be beaten just until stiff.

The mixture should be well chilled before it is put into the freezer, and the container should be filled no more than two thirds full. Air whipped in by the dasher action or during the hand beating will cause the ice cream to swell considerably.

The flavor of homemade ice cream is improved by the process called *ripening*, which is to hold the mixture frozen for a few hours after its initial freezing. To ripen ice cream made with ice and salt, remove the dasher and pack down the ice cream in the container with a spoon. Put a tight-fitting lid on the container and drain off all accumulated water around it. Repack the ice cream with a mixture of *three* parts ice to one part salt. Cover the top and sides of the inner container with this mixture and then wrap with a heavy rug or blanket. Let stand for two to four hours.

To ripen refrigerator-made ice cream, pack the frozen dessert firmly into a container and cover with a lid or a sheet of aluminum foil. Let stand in the freezer at the coldest setting at least two hours before serving.

The ice used for freezing ice cream may be purchased in markets by the block, in cubes or in crushed form. It also may be manufactured and stored ahead in your own freezer or refrigerator. Two cups of water makes about one pound of ice.

However you obtain the ice, it should be finely crushed. One way is to place it in a burlap bag and pound it with a hammer or wooden mallet. The coarse rock salt used also is called ice cream salt.

RECIPES

Here is a collection of some most popular and also rare ice cream recipes, some very old and some quite new.

Although some recipes, such as Frozen Custard and Frozen Pudding, are not ice creams by exact definition, I have included them in this category because of their popularity and their distinctive flavors and textures.

If your ingredients all must be purchased at the supermarket, some of these homemade delicacies, such as French Ice Cream, are more expensive than if bought commercially. But recipes for these have been included because of the delicious flavor and texture when homemade. They are included also for the benefit of families that have a cow to supply the cream, and a few chickens to supply the egg yolks. (The whites can be used in Angel Food Cake to serve with the ice cream.)

Most of these ice cream recipes will make a quantity suitable for freezing in a one-gallon ice cream freezer. For freezing in the refrigerator freezer area or when a smaller quantity is needed, the ingredients' amounts may be cut in half.

For recipes that have vanilla as an ingredient, vanilla beans (see instructions for using in Philadelphia Ice Cream), or pure vanilla extract should be used. Artificial vanilla flavor will not survive the freezing process and may give the ice cream an off-flavor.

ICE CREAMS

Philadelphia Ice Cream is a plain recipe, made only with rich cream, sugar and vanilla, which are mixed and then frozen. Although not as smooth as today's commercial varieties, it has a delicious, delicate flavor that is preferred by many.

PHILADELPHIA
ICE CREAM
(Vanilla)

3 quarts light cream
2 cups sugar
1 vanilla bean, broken into small pieces
   (or 2 tablespoons pure vanilla extract)
¼ teaspoon salt

Heat cream to scalding (just below boiling point, or until tiny bubbles appear around the edges). Add pieces of vanilla bean, sugar and salt, and stir until sugar is dissolved. Let stand until cool. Strain out vanilla bean and freeze. (Vanilla bean may be reused.) If used instead, the vanilla extract is added after the cream-sugar mixture has cooled.

PHILADELPHIA
ICE CREAM
(Chocolate)

3 quarts light cream
2 cups sugar
2 tablespoons pure vanilla extract
¼ teaspoon salt
3 ounces (3 squares) unsweetened chocolate, melted

Heat cream to scalding, then add sugar, salt and melted chocolate. Stir to blend thoroughly. Cool, add vanilla and freeze.

PHILADELPHIA
ICE CREAM
(Strawberry)

2½ quarts light cream
2½ cups sugar
¼ teaspoon salt
2 cups fresh strawberries

Scald cream. Add 2 cups sugar and salt. Stir to dissolve. Cool. Meanwhile, crush strawberries with potato masher or put through blender. Add remaining ½ cup sugar and blend well to dissolve sugar. Add to cooled cream mixture and freeze.

French Ice Cream is a rich, creamy dessert in which egg yolks are added to the basic cream-sugar-flavoring mixture. Because several egg yolks and a heavier cream are used, French Ice Cream is expensive, but it is one of the most popular because of its delicious flavor and smooth texture.

FRENCH ICE CREAM
(Vanilla)

1½ cups sugar
¼ teaspoon salt
12 egg yolks
2 quarts heavy cream
2 tablespoons pure vanilla extract

Add sugar and salt to egg yolks. Blend well with an egg beater, wooden spoon or in a blender. Gradually add cream until well blended. Add vanilla and freeze.

FRENCH ICE CREAM
(Chocolate)

1½ cups sugar
¼ teaspoon salt
12 egg yolks
1 cup real cocoa
¼ cup hot water
2 quarts heavy cream
2 tablespoons pure vanilla extract

Add sugar and salt to egg yolks and beat until well blended and sugar is dissolved. Add hot water to cocoa and stir to a paste. Add to egg yolk mixture and beat to combine. Gradually stir in cream and vanilla until well blended. Freeze.

12

FRENCH ICE CREAM
(Strawberry)

1½ cups sugar
¼ teaspoon salt
12 egg yolks
2 quarts heavy cream
3 cups fresh strawberries, mashed

Blend one cup sugar, salt and egg yolks. Combine mashed (or blended) strawberries and remaining ½ cup sugar. Combine with egg yolk mixture and blend well. Gradually add cream and beat to blend. Freeze.

Italian Ice Cream is a variation of the French, in which the egg whites, stiffly beaten, are added to the cream-sugar-egg yolk mixture. Since it requires less cream and fewer eggs, it is less expensive than the French version but has a very delicate, creamy consistency.

ITALIAN ICE CREAM
(Vanilla)

1 cup sugar
¼ teaspoon salt
6 egg yolks
1 quart whole milk
1 quart heavy cream
2 tablespoons pure vanilla extract
6 egg whites

Combine ½ cup sugar and salt with egg yolks. Blend well. Heat milk to scalding, then add to egg yolk mixture, stirring well to dissolve sugar and blend. Set aside to cool. Meanwhile, beat egg whites until frothy and gradually blend in remaining ½ cup sugar and continue beating until fairly stiff peaks are formed. Do not overbeat. When egg yolk mixture has cooled, fold in beaten egg whites until completely blended, then mix in cream and vanilla. Freeze.

ITALIAN ICE CREAM
(Chocolate)

1½ cups sugar
¼ teaspoon salt
6 egg yolks
3 squares (3 ounces) unsweetened chocolate, melted
1 quart whole milk
1 quart heavy cream
2 tablespoons pure vanilla extract
6 egg whites

Combine 1 cup sugar and salt with egg yolks. Blend well. Heat milk to scalding, then add chocolate, stirring well to melt chocolate and blend. Gradually add hot liquid to egg yolk mixture and blend well. Set aside to cool. Beat egg whites until frothy, then gradually blend in remaining ½ cup sugar and continue beating until peaks form, but whites are still moist. When first mixture has cooled, add vanilla and fold in egg whites until completely mixed in. Mix in cream and freeze.

15

ITALIAN ICE CREAM
(Strawberry)

1½ cups sugar
¼ teaspoon salt
6 egg yolks
1 quart whole milk
1 quart heavy cream
3 cups fresh strawberries
6 egg whites

Combine 1 cup sugar, salt and egg yolks. Beat well. Heat milk to scalding and add to egg yolk mixture. Mix well and set aside to cool. Meanwhile mash strawberries. In another bowl, beat egg whites until frothy, gradually add ½ cup sugar and continue beating until moist peaks form. When egg yolk-milk mixture has cooled, combine it with cream, mashed strawberries and egg whites. Blend well and freeze.

New York Ice Cream has many names, including French Ice Cream (which it is not), custard and cooked ice cream. It actually is a combination of several ice cream methods. This version is somewhat less expensive than French Ice Cream, but it makes a rich, creamy dessert, with good texture and flavor.

16

NEW YORK ICE CREAM
(Vanilla)

1 cup sugar
¼ teaspoon salt
6 egg yolks
1 quart whole milk
1 quart heavy cream
1 tablespoon unflavored gelatin
2 tablespoons cold water
2 tablespoons pure vanilla extract

Sprinkle gelatin over 2 tablespoons cold water in a cup. Set aside. Combine sugar, salt and egg yolks. Beat well. In another saucepan, heat milk to scalding, then add to egg yolk mixture. In a double boiler, cook mixture 5 to 10 minutes, or until it comes to a boil and coats the spoon. Remove from heat and add gelatin which has been softened in cold water. Stir well. Cool. Add cream and vanilla. Freeze.

17

NEW YORK ICE CREAM
(Chocolate)

1 cup sugar
¼ teaspoon salt
6 egg yolks
2 ounces unsweetened chocolate
   (or 1 cup real cocoa mixed with ¼ cup hot water)
1 quart whole milk
1 quart heavy cream
1 tablespoon unflavored gelatin
2 tablespoons cold water
2 tablespoons pure vanilla extract

In a cup, add the cold water to gelatin and stir to blend. Set aside. In a mixing bowl combine sugar, salt and egg yolks. Beat well. In a saucepan, heat milk to scalding, add chocolate and stir until chocolate is melted (or add cocoa mixed with hot water and stir to blend). Add egg yolk mixture and cook 5 to 10 minutes, until it comes to a boil and coats the spoon. Remove from heat and add gelatin which has been softened in cold water. Beat well. Cool. Add cream and vanilla. Freeze.

**NEW YORK ICE CREAM
(Strawberry)**

1 cup sugar
¼ teaspoon salt
6 egg yolks
1 quart whole milk
1 quart heavy cream
2 cups fresh strawberries
1 (3-ounce) package strawberry-flavored gelatin

Combine sugar, salt and egg yolks. Beat well. Mash strawberries or put through blender. In a saucepan, heat milk to scalding, then add egg yolk mixture. Cook mixture over low heat to medium heat in a double boiler 5 to 10 minutes, or until it comes to a boil and coats the spoon. Remove from heat and add gelatin. Stir well. Cool. Add strawberries and cream. Freeze.

Marlow is an inexpensive, creamy frozen dessert in which marshmallows are used to give it a creamy texture, as well as for sweetening.

MARLOW
(Vanilla)

1 pound marshmallows
3 cups whole milk
2 tablespoons pure vanilla extract
3 cups whipping cream

Heat milk to scalding. Add marshmallows and stir until they are melted. Cool, then add vanilla. Refrigerate until mixture begins to thicken. Meanwhile, whip cream until it forms soft peaks. When milk mixture is thickened, fold in whipped cream and freeze.

MARLOW
(Chocolate)

1 pound marshmallows
4 squares (4 ounces) unsweetened chocolate
3 cups whole milk
2 tablespoons pure vanilla extract
3 cups whipping cream

Heat milk to scalding. Add marshmallows and chocolate and stir until both are melted. Cool until mixture begins to thicken. Meanwhile, whip cream until it forms soft but firm peaks. Fold into milk mixture. Add vanilla and freeze.

MARLOW
(Strawberry)

1 pound marshmallows
3 cups whole milk
2 cups strawberries
   (or 1 package frozen strawberries, thawed)
¼ cup sugar
3 cups whipping cream

Heat milk to scalding. Add marshmallows and stir until marshmallows are melted. Refrigerate until mixture begins to thicken. Meanwhile, whip cream until it forms firm peaks. In another bowl, mash strawberries well and add sugar. Mix well to dissolve sugar. Fold both mixtures into milk mixture and stir well to combine. Freeze.

Frozen Custard is a rich, creamy frozen dessert, and in this recipe it is richer than the commercial variety.

FROZEN CUSTARD
(Vanilla)

1 quart milk
2 tablespoons cornstarch
1 cup sugar
½ teaspoon salt
4 egg yolks
3 cups heavy cream
2 tablespoons pure vanilla extract

Combine cornstarch, ¾ cup sugar and salt in medium-sized saucepan. Gradually add milk and cook over hot

21

water 5 to 10 minutes, or until mixture comes to a boil. Stir constantly during this time. Slightly beat egg yolks with remaining ¼ cup sugar. Add a small amount of hot mixture and stir well. Pour egg yolk mixture into cooked milk mixture and continue cooking, stirring constantly, 3 minutes more. Cool. Add cream and vanilla and freeze.

FROZEN CUSTARD (Chocolate)

1 quart milk
2 tablespoons cornstarch
¾ cup real cocoa
1½ cups sugar
¼ teaspoon salt
4 egg yolks
3 cups heavy cream
2 tablespoons pure vanilla extract

Combine cornstarch, cocoa, 1 cup sugar and salt in a saucepan. Add a small amount of milk and stir well until blended. Add remaining milk and cook over hot water 5 to 10 minutes, or until mixture comes to a boil, stirring constantly. Beat egg yolks and add remaining ½ cup sugar. Add a small amount of hot mixture to egg yolks and stir well, then pour egg yolk mixture into cooked milk mixture and continue cooking, stirring constantly, 3 minutes more. Cool. Add cream and vanilla and freeze.

FROZEN CUSTARD
(Strawberry)

1 quart milk
2 tablespoons cornstarch
1½ cups sugar
½ teaspoon salt
4 egg yolks
3 cups heavy cream
2 cups fresh (or frozen, thawed) strawberries

Combine cornstarch, one cup sugar and salt in a saucepan. Gradually add milk and cook over hot water 5 to 10 minutes, or until mixture comes to a boil. Stir constantly. Add remaining ½ cup sugar to egg yolks and beat well. Add a small amount of hot mixture to eggs and blend well, then pour egg mixture into cooked mixture and continue cooking, stirring constantly, 3 minutes more. Cool. Add cream and strawberries which have been mashed or run through blender. Freeze.

Rennet Ice Cream is made by using commercial rennet tablets (an enzyme used as a thickening agent for cheese and puddings) to give the product a creamy consistency. Rennet makes a smooth ice cream at low cost.

23

RENNET ICE CREAM
(Vanilla)

2 rennet tablets
2 tablespoons cold water
1 cup sugar
¼ teaspoon salt
1½ quarts whole milk
2 cups heavy cream
2 tablespoons pure vanilla extract

Add water to rennet and let stand to dissolve. Add sugar and salt to milk and heat to lukewarm, then add dissolved rennet. Let stand 30 minutes, or until thickened. Mix in cream and vanilla. Freeze.

RENNET ICE CREAM
(Chocolate)

2 rennet tablets
2 tablespoons cold water
1½ cups sugar
¼ teaspoon salt
¾ cup real cocoa
1½ quarts whole milk
2 cups heavy cream
2 tablespoons pure vanilla extract

Add water to rennet and let stand to dissolve. Combine cocoa, sugar and salt in saucepan. Add milk, and heat to dissolve sugar and cocoa. Cool to lukewarm, then add dissolved rennet. Let stand 30 minutes, or until thickened. Mix in cream and vanilla. Freeze.

24

RENNET ICE CREAM (Strawberry)

2 rennet tablets
2 tablespoons cold water
1½ cups sugar
¼ teaspoon salt
1½ quarts whole milk
2 cups heavy cream
2 cups fresh (or frozen, thawed) strawberries

Add water to rennet and let stand to dissolve. Add sugar and salt to milk and heat to lukewarm, stirring to dissolve sugar. Add dissolved rennet and stir well. Let it stand 30 minutes or until thickened. Mix in cream. Partially freeze. Before mixture is solidly frozen, stir in mashed strawberries. Freeze.

Gelatin Ice Cream makes use of gelatin (usually unflavored) as a stabilizer to give the desired smooth texture. Since less cream is used and usually no eggs, it is a comparatively inexpensive ice cream.

GELATIN ICE CREAM
(Vanilla)

2 tablespoons (2 envelopes) unflavored gelatin
4 tablespoons cold water
1 quart milk
1 cup sugar
¼ teaspoon salt
1 quart light cream
2 tablespoons pure vanilla extract

Add water to gelatin and set aside to soften. Meanwhile, heat milk to scalding and add sugar and salt. Stir to dissolve, then add softened gelatin and stir well. Cool. Add vanilla and cream. Freeze.

26

**GELATIN ICE CREAM
(Chocolate)**

2 tablespoons (2 envelopes) unflavored gelatin
4 tablespoons cold water
1 quart milk
¾ cup real cocoa
1½ cups sugar
¼ teaspoon salt
1 quart light cream
2 tablespoons pure vanilla extract

Add water to gelatin and set aside to soften. Meanwhile, combine cocoa, sugar and salt, mixing well. Heat milk to scalding and add to cocoa mixture. Stir well to dissolve, then add softened gelatin and stir well again. Cool. Add vanilla and cream. Freeze.

**GELATIN ICE CREAM
(Strawberry)**

2 packages strawberry-flavored gelatin dessert
¾ cup sugar
¼ teaspoon salt
1 quart milk
1 quart light cream
2 cups fresh (or frozen, thawed) strawberries, mashed

Combine gelatin, sugar and salt. Heat milk just to boiling, then add to gelatin mixture, stirring well to dissolve. Cool. Add cream and strawberries. Freeze.

Frozen Pudding is an economical frozen dessert which may be made by substituting canned evaporated milk for cream. Although it is not a true ice cream, it is an excellent and nutritious dessert. Other quick and easy substitutions can be made by using packaged instant pudding or cooked pudding mixes.

FROZEN PUDDING
(Vanilla)

4 egg yolks
1 cup sugar
¼ teaspoon salt
1 tablespoon pure vanilla extract
4 egg whites
2 large cans evaporated milk

Pour milk into 2 refrigerator trays and set in coldest part of freezer section of refrigerator. Let stand until ice crystals form around edge of trays. Meanwhile, add salt and half of sugar to slightly beaten egg yolks. Stir until sugar is dissolved. Beat egg whites until frothy, then gradually add remainder of sugar, and continue beating until moist peaks form. Fold into egg yolk mixture. When canned milk is icy, whip in chilled bowl as you would whipping cream until it is very stiff. Fold into egg mixture, add vanilla and freeze until firm.

FROZEN PUDDING
(Chocolate)

4 egg yolks
1 cup sugar
¼ teaspoon salt
1 tablespoon pure vanilla extract
½ cup real cocoa
4 egg whites
2 large cans evaporated milk

Pour milk into two refrigerator trays and set in coldest part of freezer section of refrigerator. Let set until ice crystals form around edge of trays. Meanwhile, combine cocoa, salt and ¾ cup sugar. Mix well. Add slightly beaten egg yolks and stir until sugar is dissolved. In another bowl, beat egg whites until frothy, then gradually add remaining ¼ cup sugar and continue beating until moist peaks form. Fold into egg yolk mixture. When milk is icy, whip in chilled bowl until very stiff. Fold into egg mixture, add vanilla and freeze until firm.

FROZEN PUDDING
(Strawberry)

4 egg yolks
1 cup sugar
¼ teaspoon salt
2 cups fresh (or thawed, frozen) strawberries
4 egg whites
2 large cans evaporated milk

A few hours before making pudding, pour canned milk into two refrigerator ice cube trays and chill in freezer section until ice crystals form around edge. This prepares milk for whipping.

Add salt and one ½ cup sugar to slightly beaten egg yolks. Stir to dissolve sugar. Beat egg whites until frothy, then gradually add remaining ½ cup sugar and continue beating until moist peaks form. Fold into egg yolk mixture. In a chilled bowl, whip milk until very stiff, then fold into egg mixture. Add mashed strawberries and freeze until firm.

ICE CREAM VARIATIONS

The following flavor variations may be adapted to any of the preceding methods for making ice cream, frozen custard and frozen pudding:

Almond Crisp: Substitute ½ cup brown sugar and ½ cup honey for granulated sugar in vanilla or chocolate ice cream recipe. Add ½ cup chopped, salted peanuts, 2 cups crisp rice cereal and 1 teaspoon almond extract.

Apple Butter: To vanilla ice cream mixture, add 1 cup apple butter just before freezing.

Apricot: Add 2 cups apricot pulp (from cooked, dried apricots or fresh fruit which has been cooked, then strained) to vanilla ice cream recipe just before freezing. Omit the vanilla and substitute 2 tablespoons lemon juice.

Avocado: To vanilla ice cream mixture, add 1 cup sieved avocado pulp just before freezing. Omit the vanilla and substitute 1 teaspoon lemon extract or 1 tablespoon lemon juice.

Banana: Just before freezing vanilla ice cream mixture, add the mashed pulp of 2 or 3 bananas (about 1½ cups). Stir well.

Black Walnut: Add 1 cup chopped black walnut meats to vanilla ice cream mixture.

Burnt Almond: Add 1 cup finely chopped toasted almonds to vanilla ice cream mixture.

Butter Pecan: To vanilla ice cream mixture, add ¼ cup melted butter and 1 cup chopped pecans.

Butterscotch: Substitute brown sugar for granulated sugar in vanilla ice cream recipe. Increase vanilla by 1 teaspoon.

Caramel: Partially freeze vanilla ice cream. Just before it reaches solid stage, stir in (but do not blend completely) 1 cup caramel ice cream topping. Continue freezing until solid.

Cherry-Mint: Omit vanilla from vanilla ice cream mixture. Substitute 1 teaspoon mint extract and a few drops of green food coloring. Fold in 1 cup coarsely chopped maraschino cherries or 2 cups chopped fresh berries (any variety).

Coffee: Omit vanilla in recipe for vanilla ice cream. Substitute ½ cup very strong coffee for 1 cup milk or add 1 teaspoon instant coffee powder.

Cornflake: Add 2 cups cornflakes (or other crisp cereal) to vanilla ice cream mixture.

Currant: Omit vanilla and add 1 cup currant (or blueberry) juice to vanilla ice cream mixture. Taste for sweetness.

Fruit Pudding: Proceed with vanilla ice cream recipe. Just before freezing, fold in ½ cup chopped, canned pineapple, ½ cup chopped, candied cherries and ½ cup dried, seedless currants. Freeze.

Grape: Substitute 2 cups grape juice for 2 cups milk in vanilla ice cream mixture. Omit vanilla.

Honey: Substitute honey for sugar in vanilla or chocolate ice cream mixtures.

Lemon: Omit vanilla from vanilla ice cream mixture. Substitute ½ cup lemon juice for 1 cup milk. Add grated rind of 2 lemons and a few drops of yellow food coloring. Taste for sweetness.

Macaroon: Reduce sugar by ½ cup in vanilla ice cream mixture. Just before freezing, add 1 cup crushed macaroons.

Maple: In vanilla ice cream recipe substitute maple syrup or maple sugar for granulated sugar, or use granulated sugar and 2 teaspoons maple flavoring. The amount of vanilla should remain the same.

Marble: Freeze vanilla ice cream until quite firm. Meanwhile, melt 6 ounces semi-sweet real chocolate chips in ½ cup strong coffee, stirring until smooth. Cool. Swirl into semi-frozen vanilla ice cream, making a streaked or "marbled" effect. Freeze until firm.

Nesselrode: To vanilla ice cream mixture add 1 cup mixed candied fruit and ½ cup chopped nuts.

Nougat: To vanilla ice cream mixture add ½ cup walnuts, ½ cup filberts, ½ cup almonds and ½ cup hickory nuts, all finely chopped. Substitute almond extract for one half of the vanilla.

Orange: To vanilla ice cream mixture substitute 1 cup orange juice for 1 cup milk and add 3 tablespoons lemon juice. Omit vanilla.

Orange Ambrosia: To vanilla ice cream mixture add ½ cup frozen orange juice concentrate and ½ cup shredded coconut.

Peach: To vanilla ice cream mixture add 2 cups fresh peach pulp. Increase sugar by ½ cup and substitute one half of the vanilla with 1 teaspoon almond extract.

Peanut Brittle: Just before freezing, add 1 cup crushed peanut brittle to vanilla ice cream mixture.

Peanut Butter: Add 1 cup peanut butter to vanilla or chocolate ice cream mixture.

Peppermint: Add 1 cup finely crushed peppermint candy to vanilla ice cream mixture.

Pineapple: To vanilla ice cream mixture add 2 cups well-drained, crushed pineapple (canned or fresh) and 2 tablespoons lemon juice. Omit vanilla.

Pistachio: To vanilla ice cream mixture add 1 cup chopped pistachio nuts, 1 teaspoon almond extract and a few drops of green food coloring. Retain vanilla in recipe.

Prune: Add 2 cups mashed, strained prune pulp and 2 tablespoons lemon juice to vanilla ice cream recipe. Omit vanilla.

Raspberry: Add 2 cups strained raspberry (or other berry) pulp to vanilla ice cream mixture. Add 2 tablespoons lemon juice and omit vanilla.

Tea: Omit vanilla in vanilla ice cream recipe. Substitute 1 cup strong tea for 1 cup milk.

Tutti Fruitti: Reduce vanilla amount by half in vanilla ice cream recipe. Add 1 cup crushed, drained pineapple, ½ cup chopped maraschino cherries and ½ cup chopped walnuts.

Walnut: Add 1 cup chopped walnuts to vanilla ice cream mixture.

SHERBETS

The word "sherbet" comes from the Arabic for "drink," as does our word "shrub," meaning fruit drink. There are two varieties: ice sherbet and milk (or cream) sherbet.

Ice sherbets require a stabilizer, such as gelatin or egg whites or both, to insure smoothness. *Milk sherbets* may or may not call for gelatin or egg whites.

To make either type sherbet, fruit or fruit juices are sweetened and thickened slightly with gelatin and/or with stiffly beaten egg whites, and then are frozen.

Sherbets are smoothest when they are stirred while freezing and may be frozen in an ice cream freezer, in ice cube refrigerator trays or in an electric ice cream maker placed in the freezer or freezing section of the refrigerator.

ICE SHERBETS

APRICOT SHERBET

1 tablespoon (1 envelope) unflavored gelatin
5 cups water
2 cups sugar
3 cups apricot pulp
¼ cup lemon juice
4 egg whites

Soften gelatin in ¼ cup cold water. Combine remaining water and sugar and bring to a boil, stirring constantly to

36

dissolve sugar. Add apricot pulp and softened gelatin and stir well. Chill until cold. Add lemon juice and freeze until mushy. Remove to a chilled bowl and add unbeaten egg whites. Beat until fluffy. Freeze in ice cream freezer or refrigerator freezer area. Makes 2½ quarts.

CHERRY SHERBET

1 package cherry-flavored gelatin dessert
5 cups water
1 cup sugar
4 egg whites
½ cup lemon juice
4 cups fresh cherries

Chop or grind cherries fine or run through blender with one of the five cups water. Combine remaining water and sugar and bring to a boil, stirring to dissolve sugar. Add gelatin and stir until dissolved. Add cherry pulp and chill. When cold, add lemon juice and freeze until mushy. In a chilled bowl, combine mixture with unbeaten egg whites and beat until fluffy. Freeze in ice cream freezer or refrigerator freezer area until firm. Makes 1 gallon.

CRANBERRY SHERBET

1 tablespoon (1 envelope) unflavored gelatin
3 cups water
2 cups sugar
1 cup orange juice
Grated rind of 1 orange
½ cup lemon juice
4 cups (1 pound) fresh cranberries
4 egg whites

Soften gelatin in ¼ cup cold water. Combine sugar, remaining water and cranberries and cook until sugar is dissolved and cranberries burst. Strain and add softened gelatin. Stir well to dissolve gelatin. Chill. When cold, add orange and lemon juices and rind. Freeze until mixture begins to get firm. Break up and put in chilled bowl with unbeaten egg whites. Beat until thick and fluffy. Freeze. Makes 2 quarts.

GRAPE SHERBET

1 tablespoon (1 envelope) unflavored gelatin
3 cups water
2 cups sugar
4 egg whites
3 cups grape juice (fresh, canned or reconstituted frozen)
½ cup lemon juice

Soften gelatin in ¼ cup cold water. Add remaining water to sugar and bring to a boil, stirring constantly to dissolve sugar. Add softened gelatin and stir well to dissolve gelatin. Chill until cold. Add grape and lemon juice. Freeze until mushy. Place in chilled bowl, add unbeaten egg whites and beat until fluffy. Freeze in ice cream freezer or refrigerator freeze area. Makes 2 quarts.

LEMON SHERBET

1 tablespoon (1 envelope) unflavored gelatin
5 cups cold water
2½ cups sugar
4 egg whites
1 cup lemon juice
Grated rind of 1 lemon

Soften gelatin in ¼ cup cold water. Meanwhile, add remaining water to sugar and bring to a boil. Cook two to three minutes, or until sugar is thoroughly dissolved. Add softened gelatin and stir until gelatin is dissolved. Chill thoroughly, then add lemon juice and rind. Pour into refrigerator trays or a shallow pan and place in freezer section of refrigerator until it begins to freeze. While it is still mushy, put in a chilled bowl, add unbeaten egg whites and beat until mixture is fluffy. Return to refrigerator and freeze, or freeze in ice cream freezer or electric ice cream maker in refrigerator. Makes 2 quarts.

MINT SHERBET

1 tablespoon (1 envelope) unflavored gelatin
4 cups water
½ cup chopped fresh mint
2 cups sugar
1 cup lemon juice
4 egg whites
Few drops green food coloring

Soften gelatin in ¼ cup cold water. Add remaining water to sugar and bring to a boil, stirring well to dissolve sugar. Add chopped mint, remove from heat and let steep one hour. Strain. Heat 1 cup mint water to boiling and add to gelatin mixture. Stir well to dissolve gelatin, then pour back into mint mixture. Stir well. Chill until cold. Add lemon juice and coloring to tint a light green. Freeze until mushy. Break up frozen mixture into a chilled bowl and add unbeaten egg whites. Beat until fluffy. Freeze in ice cream freezer or refrigerator freezer area. Makes about 2 quarts.

ORANGE SHERBET

1 tablespoon (1 envelope) unflavored gelatin
3 cups water
2 cups sugar
4 egg whites
3 cups orange juice (fresh or reconstituted frozen)
½ cup lemon juice
Grated rind of 1 orange

Soften gelatin in ¼ cup cold water. Mix sugar and remaining water and boil until sugar is dissolved. Add softened gelatin and stir thoroughly. Chill until cold. Add orange and lemon juices and grated rind. Freeze until mushy. In a chilled bowl, add unbeaten egg whites to frozen mixture and beat 1 minute, or until fluffy. Freeze. Makes 2 quarts.

PEACH SHERBET

Follow directions for Apricot Sherbet, substituting peach pulp for apricot pulp called for in recipe.

PINEAPPLE SHERBET

1 tablespoon (1 envelope) unflavored gelatin
4 cups water
2 cups sugar
4 egg whites
2 cups crushed unsweetened pineapple
2 tablespoons lemon juice

Soften gelatin in ¼ cup cold water. Mix remaining water and sugar and bring to a boil, stirring to dissolve sugar. Add softened gelatin and continue stirring until gelatin is dissolved. Chill. Add pineapple and lemon juice and partially freeze in freezer section of refrigerator. Break up in a chilled bowl, add egg whites (unbeaten) and beat until mixture is thick and fluffy. Freeze. Makes 2 quarts.

RASPBERRY SHERBET

1 tablespoon (1 envelope) unflavored gelatin
5 cups cold water
2 cups sugar
¼ cup lemon juice
4 egg whites
4 cups fresh or frozen raspberries

Soften gelatin in ¼ cup cold water. Combine remaining water, sugar and raspberries in a saucepan and bring to a boil, stirring constantly. Lower heat and simmer until sugar is dissolved and raspberries are soft. Strain and add softened gelatin. Stir to dissolve gelatin. Chill until cold, then add lemon juice and freeze until mushy. Remove to a chilled bowl, add unbeaten egg whites and beat until fluffy. Freeze until firm in ice cream freezer or refrigerator freezer area. Makes 2 quarts.

**RHUBARB
SHERBET**

1 tablespoon (1 envelope) unflavored gelatin
4 cups diced rhubarb
2½ cups water
2 cups sugar
4 egg whites

Soften gelatin in ½ cup cold water. Add remaining water to rhubarb and slowly bring to a boil. Simmer, stirring occasionally, over low heat until rhubarb is well cooked. Strain, add sugar to liquid and stir until sugar is dissolved. Remove from heat and add softened gelatin. Chill until cold, then freeze to the mushy stage. Remove to a chilled bowl and add egg whites, unbeaten. Beat until fluffy, then return to freezer or freeze in an ice cream freezer. Makes 2 quarts.

STRAWBERRY SHERBET

1 package strawberry-flavored gelatin dessert
5 cups water
1½ cups sugar
4 egg whites
4 cups fresh or frozen strawberries

Combine sugar and water. Bring to a boil, stirring well to dissolve sugar. Add gelatin and stir to dissolve. Chill until cold. Meanwhile mash strawberries or run through blender to make a thick pulp. Add to cold gelatin mixture and freeze until mushy. In a chilled bowl, add unbeaten egg whites and beat until fluffy. Freeze in ice cream freezer or refrigerator freezer area. Makes 2½ quarts.

TUTTI FRUITTI SHERBET

1 teaspoon (1 envelope) unflavored gelatin
6 cups water
6 medium-sized oranges
2 cups sugar
Juice of 1 lemon
4 egg whites

Soften gelatin in ¼ cup cold water. Add one cup water to the sugar and bring to a boil. Meanwhile, peel and section three of the oranges. Remove any seeds. One at a time, drop the orange sections into the boiling syrup and simmer until transparent. While they cook, one at a time, juice the three remaining oranges and the lemon. Finely grate the rind of the oranges and lemon. As they are cooked, dip out the orange sections and set aside to drain and cool. When all are cooked, add the remaining water, the dissolved gelatin, the juices and grated rind to the syrup in which the orange sections have been cooked. Freeze almost solid, then break up and beat with the unbeaten egg whites in a chilled bowl. Freeze until almost firm. Add orange sections and freeze. Makes 2 quarts.

WATERMELON SHERBET

1 tablespoon (1 envelope) unflavored gelatin
5 cups watermelon juice (pressed from fresh melon)
2 cups sugar
½ cup lemon juice
4 egg whites
Few drops red food coloring

Soften gelatin in ½ cup juice. Heat remaining juice to boiling, then add sugar and stir until sugar is dissolved. Add softened gelatin. Chill. Add lemon juice and enough coloring to make it a delicate pink. Freeze until mushy. Place mixture and unbeaten egg whites in a chilled bowl and beat until frothy. Freeze until firm in ice cream freezer or refrigerator freezer area. Makes about 1½ quarts.

MILK SHERBETS

Milk sherbets are made much the same as water sherbets except that milk or cream is used in place of the gelatin as a stabilizer. Egg whites may or may not be used. Milk sherbets are richer in flavor and higher in calories than water sherbets but are not as rich (or as calorie-laden) as ice creams.

APRICOT SHERBET

4 cups apricot juice
1 cup water
1 cup light cream
1 cup sugar
3 tablespoons lemon juice
4 egg whites

Cook water and sugar until sugar is dissolved. Add apricot juice and cool. Add lemon juice and cream. Freeze until mushy. Remove to a chilled bowl and add unbeaten egg whites, then beat until light. Freeze until firm. Makes 2 quarts.

BUTTERMILK SHERBET

4 cups buttermilk
1 cup sugar
3 cups crushed unsweetened pineapple
2 egg whites
3 teaspoons pure vanilla extract

Combine buttermilk, sugar and pineapple and let stand until sugar is dissolved. Freeze to mushy stage. Remove to a chilled bowl, add unbeaten egg whites and vanilla and beat until light and fluffy. Freeze. Makes 2 quarts.

CITRUS SHERBET

4 cups milk
2 cups light cream
2 cups sugar
2 cups orange juice
¼ cup lemon juice
2 cups crushed unsweetened pineapple, with juice

Heat two cups milk to scalding. Remove from heat, add sugar and stir until dissolved. Add remaining ingredients and freeze in ice cream freezer or in freezer section. If frozen in the refrigerator, partially freeze mixture, then remove to chilled bowl and beat until soft, then return to freezer and freeze until firm. Makes 2 quarts.

**GRAPE
SHERBET**

2 cups grape juice
6 cups milk
½ cup lemon juice
1½ cups sugar

Heat grape juice and add sugar. Stir to dissolve. Add milk, then lemon juice. Chill, then freeze. Makes 2 quarts.

**LEMON CREAM
SHERBET**

4 cups milk
2 cups light cream
2½ cups sugar
2 cups lemon juice

Heat two cups milk to scalding. Remove from heat. Add sugar and stir until dissolved. Add remaining ingredients. Freeze in ice cream freezer or in freezer section of refrigerator. If frozen in ice cube trays, the mixture should be partially frozen, then removed, beaten until fluffy and returned to complete the freezing. Makes 2½ quarts.

ORANGE SHERBET

Juice of 10 oranges
Juice of 2 lemons
2 cups sugar
2 cups whipping cream

Mix sugar and juices and let stand until sugar is dissolved. Whip cream and fold into sweetened juices. Freeze. Makes 1½ quarts.

YOGURT SHERBET

A delicious, healthful sherbet may be made by adding one cup sweetened fruit to each quart of homemade or commercial yogurt. Freeze without beating.

WATER ICES

Water ices are simple, easy-to-make desserts made by freezing sweetened, diluted fruit juice. Ices should be stirred at least once or twice during the freezing process.

APRICOT ICE

4 cups apricot juice
2 cups water
1½ cups sugar

Heat water to boiling, add sugar and stir to dissolve. Chill. Add apricot juice and freeze. Makes 2 quarts.

CIDER ICE

4 cups apple cider
1½ cups water
1½ cups sugar
¼ cup lemon juice

Heat water to boiling, add sugar and stir to dissolve. Cool. Add cider and juice. Freeze. Makes 2 quarts.

50

COLA ICE

2 cups water
2 (8-ounce) bottles cola drink
½ cup lemon juice
¾ cup sugar

Heat water to boiling. Add sugar and stir to dissolve. Cool. Add lemon juice and cola. Freeze.

CRANBERRY ICE

4 cups water
2½ cups sugar
4 cups cranberries

Add cranberries and sugar to water and bring to a boil, stirring to dissolve sugar. Cook until cranberries burst, then press through a sieve. Chill, then freeze. Makes 2 quarts.

GINGER ALE ICE

2 cups water
2 (8-ounce) bottles ginger ale
1 cup orange juice
½ cup lemon juice
¾ cup sugar

Combine sugar and water and heat until sugar is dissolved. Chill, then add remaining ingredients. Freeze. Makes 1½ quarts.

**GRAPEFRUIT
ICE**

2 cups grapefruit juice
1 cup water
1 cup sugar

Add sugar to water and bring to a boil. Stir to dissolve. Chill. Add grapefruit juice and freeze. Makes 1 quart.

**LEMON
ICE**

4 cups water
2 cups sugar
1 cup lemon juice

Heat water and sugar until sugar is dissolved. Chill. Add lemon juice and freeze. Makes 1½ quarts.

**MIXED FRUIT
ICE**

2 bananas
2 cups apricot juice
Juice of 3 lemons
Juice of 3 oranges
2 cups sugar
3 cups water

Mash bananas. Add juices. Dissolve sugar in water which has been heated to boiling. Chill. Add to fruit mixture and freeze. Makes 2 quarts.

ORANGE ICE

4 cups water
2 cups sugar
2 cups orange juice
Grated rind of one orange
¼ cup lemon juice

Add sugar to water and heat, stirring, until sugar is dissolved. Chill. Add juices and rind. Freeze in ice cream freezer or refrigerator freezer area. Makes 2 quarts.

PINEAPPLE ICE

5 cups water
¼ cup lemon juice
1½ cups sugar
2 cups crushed unsweetened pineapple, with juice

Heat two cups water to boiling. Add sugar and stir to dissolve. Chill. Add lemon juice, remaining water and pineapple and freeze. Makes 2 quarts.

RASPBERRY-CURRANT ICE

2 quarts currants
2 quarts raspberries
3 cups sugar
2 cups water

Put currants and raspberries in two bowls. Over each sprinkle one cup sugar. Let set one hour, then stir well and leave overnight. Stir again and strain juice into bowl. You should have 2½ cups currant juice and 1½ cups raspberry juice. Dissolve the remaining sugar in the water, which has been heated to boiling. Cool, then add juices. Freeze. Makes 2 quarts.

ROOT BEER
ICE

1 (8-ounce) bottle root beer
1 tablespoon lemon juice
1 tablespoon sugar

Combine all ingredients. Stir to dissolve sugar. Freeze. Makes two servings.

PARFAITS

The base of a parfait is a mixture of beaten eggs or egg whites into which a hot, cooked syrup is beaten. Whipped cream and fruits are folded in. A parfait is frozen in a mold and without stirring during the freezing process.

BANANA PARFAIT

½ cup sugar
½ cup water
2 egg whites
1 teaspoon lemon juice
1 cup mashed ripe banana
1½ cups whipping cream

Boil sugar and water until it reaches soft ball stage (238 degrees). Meanwhile, beat egg whites until they form stiff peaks. Stirring constantly, gradually pour a stream of the syrup into the beaten egg whites. Beat until cool and stiff. Add lemon juice and banana. Fold in cream which has been whipped stiff. Freeze. Makes 1 quart.

CHOCOLATE PARFAIT

1 cup sugar
½ cup water
2 squares (2 ounces) unsweetened chocolate
2 egg whites
3 teaspoons pure vanilla extract
1½ cups whipping cream

Boil sugar and water until it reaches soft ball stage (238 degrees). Add chocolate to hot syrup and stir until chocolate dissolves. Beat egg whites until they form stiff peaks. Gradually pour the chocolate-syrup mixture in a stream into the beaten egg whites, beating constantly. Beat until cool and stiff. Add vanilla and fold in cream which has been whipped until stiff. Freeze. Makes 1½ quarts.

COCONUT PARFAIT

½ cup sugar
½ cup water
2 egg whites
3 teaspoons pure vanilla extract
½ cup toasted coconut
1½ cups whipping cream

Cook sugar and water to 238 degrees (soft ball stage). Meanwhile, beat egg whites until they form stiff peaks, then pour syrup into the egg whites, beating constantly. Beat until mixture is cool and stiff. Add vanilla and coconut. Fold in cream which has been whipped until stiff. Freeze. Makes 1½ quarts.

COFFEE PARFAIT

¾ cup strong coffee
¾ cup sugar
2 egg whites
3 teaspoons pure vanilla extract
1½ cups whipping cream

Add sugar to coffee and bring to a boil. Cook over high heat until syrup reaches 238 degrees (soft ball stage).

Meanwhile, beat egg whites to stiff peaks, then pour a stream of the syrup, beating constantly, into the beaten egg whites. Beat until cool and stiff. Add vanilla and fold in cream which has been whipped until stiff. Freeze. Makes 1½ quarts.

MAPLE PARFAIT

4 eggs
2 cups whipping cream
1 cup maple syrup
⅛ teaspoon salt

Add salt to eggs and beat until yolks and whites are well blended. Heat syrup to boiling and pour in a steady stream, beating constantly, into the beaten eggs. Cook in a double boiler until thick. Cool. Fold in cream which has been whipped until stiff. Fill mold. Freeze without stirring. Makes 2 quarts.

PINEAPPLE-MINT PARFAIT

1 cup sugar
1½ cups crushed unsweetened pineapple
1½ cups whipping cream
½ cup water
2 egg whites
½ teaspoon mint flavoring

Add sugar to water and bring to a boil. Cook to soft ball stage (238 degrees). Beat egg whites until they form stiff

57

peaks, then slowly pour syrup over them, beating constantly. Fold in pineapple and add mint flavoring. Lastly add cream which has been whipped until stiff. Fill mold and freeze. Garnish with fresh mint leaves. Makes 1½ quarts.

QUICK CRANBERRY PARFAIT

2 cups (1 can) jellied cranberry sauce
6 tablespoons sugar
2 egg whites
1 cup whipping cream

Beat egg whites until stiff. Gradually add sugar while continuing to beat. Gently fold into the cranberry sauce which has been broken with a fork. Fold in cream which has been whipped until stiff. Freeze. Makes 2 quarts.

PEPPERMINT PARFAIT

½ cup sugar
½ cup water
2 egg whites
2 cups whipping cream
½ cup crushed peppermint candy

Combine sugar and water and bring to a boil. Cook until syrup reaches soft ball stage (238 degrees). Meanwhile, beat egg whites to stiff peaks. Pour syrup slowly into egg whites, beating constantly. Chill. Fold in crushed candy, then cream which has been whipped until stiff. Freeze. Makes 1½ quarts.

PISTACHIO PARFAIT

1 cup sugar
¼ cup water
2 egg whites
½ cup pistachio nuts
1 teaspoon almond extract
2 cups whipping cream
Salt
Few drops green food coloring

Combine sugar and water. Heat to boiling, then cook to 238 degrees (soft ball stage). Beat egg whites stiff, then gradually pour in syrup, beating constantly. Tint a light green. Cool, then add chopped nuts, almond extract and a pinch of salt. Fold in cream which has been whipped stiff. Freeze. Makes 1½ quarts.

STRAWBERRY PARFAIT

1 cup sugar
1½ cups crushed strawberries
1½ cups whipping cream
½ cup water
2 egg whites

Combine sugar and water. Bring to a boil, then cook to soft ball stage (238 degrees). Beating constantly, pour in a steady stream over the stiffly beaten egg whites. Continue beating until cold. Fold in crushed strawberries, then carefully fold in stiffly whipped cream. Fill mold and freeze. Makes 1½ quarts.

59

VANILLA PARFAIT

½ cup sugar
½ cup water
2 egg whites
3 teaspoons pure vanilla extract
1½ cups whipping cream

Boil sugar and water to the soft ball stage (238 degrees). Beat egg whites until they form stiff peaks. Gradually pour a stream of the syrup into beaten egg whites, beating constantly. Beat until mixture is cool and holds its shape. Add vanilla. Fold in cream which has been whipped stiff. Freeze. Makes 1 quart.

MOUSSE

A mousse is made by folding fruits or flavorings into sweetened whipped cream. It is frozen as a mold, without stirring. An ice cream freezer with agitator is not used.

The traditional method of freezing a mousse in salt and ice is to pour the mixture into a mold or container, then cover it with waxed paper and place a tight-fitting cover over the paper. The container then is sealed to keep the brine from seeping into the cream mixture. This can be done by winding a piece of adhesive tape around the edge or tying it with a cloth dipped in paraffin around the lower edge of the cover.

The container is then buried in a mixture of one part crushed ice to one part salt. Let set for at least four hours, draining off the liquid as the ice melts and adding more salt and ice mixture as necessary.

A mousse also may be frozen in the freezer section of the refrigerator or in the home food freezer, but quick freezing is important to keep large crystals from forming. The freezer temperature should be set to its lowest point at least one hour before adding the mousse.

To serve, dip the container in warm water for a few seconds or wrap it in a cloth wrung out in hot water. Remove the lid and invert the container over the serving dish, the mousse having been frozen upside down in the mold.

CHOCOLATE MOUSSE

1 cup milk
¾ cup sugar
1 teaspoon unflavored gelatin
2 squares (2 ounces) unsweetened chocolate
1 teaspoon real vanilla extract
2 cups whipping cream

Add gelatin to milk. Let set 5 minutes. Slowly heat milk to scalding over hot water, stirring to dissolve gelatin. Add sugar and chocolate. Stir until chocolate is melted and all is well blended. Let cool, then add vanilla. Freeze to a mushy consistency in refrigerator tray. Remove to chilled bowl and beat until light. Meanwhile, whip cream until stiff peaks form. Fold frozen mixture into whipped cream. Pack in a mold and freeze until firm — two or three hours. Makes 1 quart.

VANILLA MOUSSE

2 egg whites
½ cup powdered sugar
2 cups whipping cream
1½ teaspoons real vanilla extract

Beat egg whites until stiff, gradually adding ¼ cup powdered sugar. Whip the cream to soft peaks, adding remaining ¼ cup sugar after peaks form. Stir in vanilla. Fold the two mixtures together, pour into mold and freeze three hours, or until firm. Makes 1 quart.

APPLESAUCE MOUSSE

2 cups whipping cream
½ cup sugar
2 cups applesauce (sweetened or unsweetened)
½ teaspoon cinnamon

Whip cream until stiff. Gradually fold in sugar, applesauce and cinnamon. Freeze. Makes 1 quart.

CARAMEL MOUSSE

½ cup sugar, caramelized
½ cup boiling water
3 egg yolks
4 tablespoons light cream
1 tablespoon butter
Pinch of salt
¾ cup whipping cream
1 teaspoon pure vanilla extract

Heat sugar in heavy skillet over low heat until it is a golden brown color. Stirring, add water and increase heat to medium. Cook, stirring constantly, until the syrup is slightly thickened. Cool to lukewarm. Beat egg yolks until thick. Add light cream and pour in syrup, stirring constantly. Return all to the skillet and cook two minutes over low heat, stirring, until the custard is smooth and thickened. Take from heat and add butter and salt. Cool. Meanwhile, whip cream until stiff. Fold chilled custard into the whipped cream. Add vanilla and freeze. Makes 1 quart.

CHERRY MOUSSE

2 cups whipping cream
½ teaspoon almond extract
½ cup sugar
1 cup canned or frozen cherries or fresh cherries

Chop cherries and mix with sugar. Let stand to dissolve sugar. Whip cream stiff, then fold in cherry mixture and extract. Freeze. Makes about 1 quart.

COCONUT-ORANGE MOUSSE

1 cup orange juice
½ cup shredded coconut
1/3 cup honey
1 cup whipping cream
2 tablespoons lemon juice

Do not strain orange juice, but pick out seeds. Add coconut and honey to juices and leave overnight in a cold place. Whip cream to stiff peaks and quickly fold in juice-coconut mixture. Freeze. Makes 1 quart.

FIG MOUSSE

2 cups whipping cream
½ cup sugar
¼ cup lemon juice
1 cup chopped figs

Whip cream to stiff peaks. Fold in sugar, then lemon juice, then figs. Freeze. Makes about 1 quart.

LEMON MOUSSE

2 cups whipping cream
½ cup sugar
½ cup lemon juice

Whip cream until stiff. Fold in sugar and add lemon juice. Freeze. Makes four servings.

MOLASSES MOUSSE

2 cups whipping cream
½ cup mild molasses
2 tablespoons orange juice
½ teaspoon cinnamon
Pinch salt
4 eggs

Beat eggs. Add molasses. Cook over hot water, stirring constantly, until thickened. Cool. Add orange juice, cinnamon and salt. Beat cream until stiff. Fold in molasses mixture and freeze. Makes about 1 quart.

PERSIMMON MOUSSE

1 cup whipping cream
½ cup sugar
1½ cups ripe persimmon pulp
¼ cup orange pulp
½ cup diced unsweetened pineapple

Combine persimmon pulp, orange and pineapple and sugar. Let stand a few minutes to dissolve sugar. Fold into cream which has been whipped to stiff peaks. Freeze. Makes four servings.

PINEAPPLE-ORANGE MOUSSE

¾ cup orange juice
¾ cup unsweetened pineapple juice
¼ cup lemon juice
1 cup crushed unsweetened pineapple
½ cup sugar
2 cups whipping cream

Combine fruit and juices and sugar. Let stand to dissolve sugar. Partially freeze to mushy stage. Fold in cream which has been whipped to stiff peaks. Freeze. Makes 1½ quarts.

RASPBERRY MOUSSE

2 cups whipping cream
1 cup sugar
1 quart raspberries

Mix raspberries and sugar. Let stand one hour to dissolve sugar. Press through sieve. Whip cream until stiff and fold in berry pulp. Freeze. Makes 1 quart.

STRAWBERRY MOUSSE

½ cup sugar
1 cup whipping cream
1 cup crushed fresh strawberries
2 egg whites

Combine sugar and strawberries and stir until sugar is dissolved. Whip cream to stiff peaks. In another bowl, beat egg whites until stiff. Fold cream into strawberries, then fold in beaten egg whites. Freeze. Makes 1 quart.

SPECIAL FROZEN DESSERTS

There is no more perfect ending to a really special meal than a Frozen Bombe, a Biscuit Tortoni or a Molded Spumone.

These aristocrats of the ice cream family look as though the cook spent hours in the kitchen for her guests' pleasure. And they taste elegantly expensive. But they aren't as difficult or as costly as they appear.

BAKED ALASKA

1 (9-inch) layer of sponge or layer cake
6 egg whites
Pinch of salt
½ cup sugar
3 to 4 cups homemade ice cream
    molded in an 8-inch cake pan

Cover a thick wooden cutting board with a piece of brown wrapping paper. Remove cake layer from pan and place on paper. Make a meringue by beating egg whites until foamy, then adding salt and small amount of sugar. Continue beating, gradually adding more sugar, until stiff peaks form and sugar is all used.

Center ice cream layer on top of cake layer and spread meringue over entire surface of ice cream and cake, being careful to seal to edge of cake. Sprinkle the top with chopped nuts, if desired.

Bake in 450-degree oven about five minutes, or until lightly browned. Serve immediately.

STRAWBERRY BOMBE

Crust:
> ¼ cup butter or margarine
> ¼ cup sugar
> 25 vanilla wafers

Soften butter at room temperature. Blend in sugar and crumbs made by crushing vanilla wafers with a rolling pin or running through blender. Pat crumb mixture onto bottom and sides of a one-quart mixing bowl, pressing the mixture in place with a smaller bowl. Refrigerate, leaving smaller bowl to hold crumbs in place.

Filling:
> 1 pint whipping cream
> ½ cup sugar
> 1 pint fresh strawberries, sliced and drained

Whip cream until it begins to thicken. Gradually add sugar and continue whipping until cream forms soft peaks, but do not overbeat. Gently fold in drained, sliced strawberries. Remove smaller bowl and pour mixture into crumb crust in larger bowl. Cover and freeze until solid, without stirring, 6 to 8 hours. To serve, unmold upside down on a serving plate and garnish with whipped cream and strawberry halves.

FROZEN BRULE

2 cups sugar
½ cup boiling water
2 tablespoons cornstarch
1½ cups milk
2 egg yolks
1 cup whipping cream

Heat sugar in iron skillet over low heat until it browns slightly. Add water and cook until all sugar is dissolved. In a double boiler, add milk to cornstarch, stirring well to blend. Add syrup and cook over hot water 15 minutes, stirring constantly. Slightly beat egg yolks in a small bowl, then add small amount of hot mixture. Stir well, then add egg mixture to hot milk mixture in double boiler. Cook two minutes more. Chill until cold. Meanwhile whip cream until it forms soft peaks. Fold into cold milk mixture and pour into mold. Freeze 6 to 8 hours, or until firm and ripened.

FROZEN PLUM PUDDING

½ cup milk
½ cup sugar
2 squares (2 ounces) unsweetened chocolate
2 cups whipping cream
1 teaspoon pure vanilla extract
½ cup chopped nuts
¼ cup maraschino cherries
1 cup seedless raisins
¼ cup chopped dates

Heat milk in saucepan. Add sugar and chocolate and heat until sugar is dissolved, chocolate is melted and the mixture is slightly thickened. Refrigerate to chill. Plump the raisins and dates by steaming for 5 minutes in a small amount of water. Cook just long enough to evaporate water, then cool. Chop nuts, cherries, raisins and dates. Mix well together. Whip cream until it forms soft peaks but is not stiff. Add vanilla, then chocolate mixture, then chopped fruits and nuts. Pour into a mold and freeze 6 to 8 hours.

SPUMONE

½ cup sugar
½ cup maraschino cherries, drained
3 tablespoons candied orange peel
1 teaspoon lemon juice
1 cup whipping cream
½ cup chopped almonds
1½ quarts homemade ice cream
¼ teaspoon almond extract

Whip cream to soft peaks. Gradually add sugar while beating. Add cherries, which have been chopped, and orange peel, which has been cut into thin strips. Add lemon juice and put into refrigerator trays to freeze. Add chopped nuts to slightly softened ice cream. Stir in almond extract.

Line the bottom and sides of a one-quart mold with ice cream mixture. Fill the mold with the whipped-cream mixture. Cover tightly and freeze 24 hours. To serve, unmold on serving plate and cut into one-inch slices.

BISCUIT TORTONI

1 tablespoon (1 envelope) unflavored gelatin
½ cup cold water
½ cup sugar
2 egg yolks
¼ teaspoon salt
1 teaspoon pure vanilla extract
½ teaspoon almond extract
1 cup whipping cream
¼ cup chopped pistachio nuts
½ cup vanilla wafer crumbs

Add ¼ cup cold water to gelatin and let stand to soften. Stir sugar into mixture and heat remaining ¼ cup water to boiling. Pour hot water into sugar-gelatin mixture and stir until dissolved.

In a bowl, beat egg yolks and salt until light and fluffy. Gradually add sugar-gelatin mixture, beating well. Chill. Meanwhile, whip cream until it forms soft peaks and fold into the chilled mixture. Stir in flavorings. Add pistachio nuts and pour into small fluted Tortoni paper cups. Sprinkle tops with crumbs. Freeze until firm.

INDEX